Congressional Research Service

Informing the legislative debate since 1914

Navy Virginia (SSN-774) Class Attack Submarine Procurement: Background and Issues for Congress

Ronald O'Rourke

Specialist in Naval Affairs

February 3, 2014

Congressional Research Service

7-5700

www.crs.gov

RL32418

Summary

The Navy has been procuring Virginia (SSN-774) class nuclear-powered attack submarines since FY1998. The two Virginia-class boats requested for FY2014 are to be the 19th and 20th boats in the class, and the first two in a 10-boat Virginia class multiyear-procurement (MYP) contract for the period FY2014-FY2018. Congress granted authority for this MYP contract as part of its action on the FY2013 Department of Defense (DOD) budget. The Navy's FY2013 budget submission had projected one Virginia-class boat in FY2014. Congress, as part of its action on the FY2013 DOD budget, added AP funding in FY2013 to support the procurement of a second Virginia-class boat in FY2014. The Navy's inclusion of a second Virginia-class boat in FY2014 (which increases from 9 to 10 the number of boats in the FY2014-FY2018 MYP contract) follows through on this congressional action.

The Navy's proposed FY2014 budget estimates the combined procurement cost of the two boats requested for FY2014 at $5,414.2 million. The two boats have received a total of $1,530.8 million in prior-year advance procurement (AP) funding (although this figure may be reduced by the March 1, 2013, sequester), leaving another $3,883.4 million to complete the funding for the two boats.

The Navy's proposed FY2014 budget requested $5,285.3 million in procurement and AP funding for the Virginia class program. This figure includes:

- $2,930.7 million in procurement funding to complete the procurement cost of the first boat requested for FY2014, and to pay part of the procurement cost of the second boat requested for FY2014;

- $1,612.0 million in AP funding for Virginia-class boats to be procured in future fiscal years; and

- $742.6 million in AP funding for Economic Order Quantity (EOQ) purchases (i.e., batch orders) of selected components of the 10 Virginia-class boats to be procured under the FY2014-FY2018 MYP contract. EOQ purchases are a regular feature of the first year or two or an MYP contract.

The Navy proposed to defer to FY2015 the remaining $952.7 million of the procurement cost of the second boat requested for FY2014. This would divide the procurement funding for the boat between two fiscal years (FY2014 and FY2015)—a funding profile sometimes called split funding. In recent instances where split funding has been used to fund Navy ships, the funding has been appropriated using a funding method called incremental funding, under which Congress takes a positive action to approve each of the two annual funding increments. For the second Virginia-class boat requested for FY2014, however, the Navy proposed using a different funding method called advance appropriations, which is a form of full funding that resembles a legislatively locked in form of incremental funding. Under advance appropriations (which is not to be confused with advance procurement [AP] funding), the FY2015 funding increment for the boat would be legislatively locked into place (i.e., it would be "automatic"), and Congress would need to take action to stop that increment from being appropriated. Although the Navy in recent years has occasionally expressed interest in using advance appropriations for funding ships, there is little precedent in recent years for funding Navy ships with advance appropriations.

DOD and the Navy are considering whether to build Virginia-class boats procured in FY2019 and subsequent years with an additional mid-body section, called the Virginia Payload Module

(VPM), that contains four large-diameter, vertical launch tubes that the boats would use to store and fire additional Tomahawk cruise missiles or other payloads, such as large-diameter unmanned underwater vehicles (UUVs). The Navy estimates that building Virginia-class boats with the VPM might increase their unit procurement costs by about 13%. It would increase the total number of torpedo-sized weapons (such as Tomahawks) that they could carry by about 76%.

The Navy's FY2014 30-year SSN procurement plan, if implemented, would not be sufficient to maintain a force of 48 SSNs consistently over the long run. The Navy projects under that plan that the SSN force would fall below 48 boats starting in FY2025, reach a minimum of 42 boats in FY2029, and remain below 48 boats through FY2034.

Potential issues for Congress regarding the Virginia-class program include the following:

- the impact on the Virginia-class program of the March 1, 2013, sequester on FY2013 funding and unobligated prior-year funding for the program;

- whether to use traditional (i.e., single-year) full funding, incremental funding, or (as the Navy proposes) advance appropriations for funding the second of the two boats requested for procurement in FY2014;

- the Virginia-class procurement rate more generally in coming years, particularly in the context of an SSN shortfall projected for FY2025-FY2034 and the larger debate over future U.S. defense strategy and defense spending; and

- Virginia-class program issues raised in a December 2012 report from DOD's Director, Operational Test and Evaluation (DOT&E).

The Navy's Ohio Replacement (SSBN[X]) ballistic missile submarine program is discussed in CRS Report R41129, *Navy Ohio Replacement (SSBN[X]) Ballistic Missile Submarine Program: Background and Issues for Congress*, by Ronald O'Rourke.

Contents

Figures

Tables

Appendixes

Contacts

Introduction

This report provides background information and issues for Congress on the Virginia-class nuclear-powered attack submarine (SSN) program. The Navy's proposed FY2014 budget requested $5,285.3 million in procurement and advance procurement (AP) funding for the program. Decisions that Congress makes on procurement of Virginia-class boats could substantially affect U.S. Navy capabilities and funding requirements, and the U.S. shipbuilding industrial base.

The Navy's Ohio Replacement (SSBN[X]) ballistic missile submarine program is discussed in another CRS report.[1]

Background

U.S. Navy Submarines[2]

The U.S. Navy operates three types of submarines—nuclear-powered ballistic missile submarines (SSBNs),[3] nuclear-powered cruise missile and special operations forces (SOF) submarines (SSGNs),[4] and nuclear-powered attack submarines (SSNs). The SSNs are general-purpose submarines that perform a variety of peacetime and wartime missions, including the following:

- covert intelligence, surveillance, and reconnaissance (ISR), much of it done for national-level (as opposed to purely Navy) purposes;

- covert insertion and recovery of SOF (on a smaller scale than possible with the SSGNs);

- covert strikes against land targets with the Tomahawk cruise missiles (again on a smaller scale than possible with the SSGNs);

---

[1] See CRS Report R41129, *Navy Ohio Replacement (SSBN[X]) Ballistic Missile Submarine Program: Background and Issues for Congress*, by Ronald O'Rourke.

[2] In U.S. Navy submarine designations, SS stands for submarine, N stands for nuclear-powered, B stands for ballistic missile, and G stands for guided missile (such as a cruise missile). Submarines can be powered by either nuclear reactors or non-nuclear power sources such as diesel engines or fuel cells. All U.S. Navy submarines are nuclear-powered. A submarine's use of nuclear or non-nuclear power as its energy source is not an indication of whether it is armed with nuclear weapons—a nuclear-powered submarine can lack nuclear weapons, and a non-nuclear-powered submarine can be armed with nuclear weapons.

[3] The SSBNs' basic mission is to remain hidden at sea with their nuclear-armed submarine-launched ballistic missiles (SLBMs) and thereby deter a strategic nuclear attack on the United States. The Navy's SSBNs are discussed in CRS Report R41129, *Navy Ohio Replacement (SSBN[X]) Ballistic Missile Submarine Program: Background and Issues for Congress*, by Ronald O'Rourke, and CRS Report RL31623, *U.S. Nuclear Weapons: Changes in Policy and Force Structure*, by Amy F. Woolf.

[4] The Navy's four SSGNs are former Trident SSBNs that have been converted (i.e., modified) to carry Tomahawk cruise missiles and SOF rather than SLBMs. Although the SSGNs differ somewhat from SSNs in terms of mission orientation (with the SSGNs being strongly oriented toward Tomahawk strikes and SOF support, while the SSNs are more general-purpose in orientation), SSGNs can perform other submarine missions and are sometimes included in counts of the projected total number of Navy attack submarines. The Navy's SSGNs are discussed in CRS Report RS21007, *Navy Trident Submarine Conversion (SSGN) Program: Background and Issues for Congress*, by Ronald O'Rourke.

- covert offensive and defensive mine warfare;
- anti-submarine warfare (ASW); and
- anti-surface ship warfare.

During the Cold War, ASW against the Soviet submarine force was the primary stated mission of U.S. SSNs, although covert ISR and covert SOF insertion/recovery operations were reportedly important on a day-to-day basis as well.[5] In the post-Cold War era, although anti-submarine warfare remains a mission, the SSN force has focused more on performing the other missions noted on the list above.

Attack Submarine Force Levels

Force-Level Goal

The Navy wants to achieve and maintain a fleet in coming years of 306 ships, including 48 SSNs.[6] For a review of SSN force level goals since the Reagan Administration, see **Appendix A**.

Force Level at End of FY2013

The SSN force included more than 90 boats during most of the 1980s, when plans called for achieving a 600-ship Navy including 100 SSNs. The number of SSNs peaked at 98 boats at the end of FY1987 and has declined since then in a manner that has roughly paralleled the decline in the total size of the Navy over the same time period. The 54 SSNs in service at the end of FY2013 included the following:

- 41 Los Angeles (SSN-688) class boats;
- 3 Seawolf (SSN-21) class boats; and
- 10 Virginia (SSN-774) class boats.

Los Angeles- and Seawolf-Class Boats

A total of 62 Los Angeles-class submarines, commonly called 688s, were procured between FY1970 and FY1990 and entered service between 1976 and 1996. They are equipped with four 21-inch diameter torpedo tubes and can carry a total of 26 torpedoes or Tomahawk cruise missiles in their torpedo tubes and internal magazines. The final 31 boats in the class (SSN-719 and higher) are equipped with an additional 12 vertical launch system (VLS) tubes in their bows for carrying and launching another 12 Tomahawk cruise missiles. The final 23 boats in the class (SSN-751 and higher) incorporate further improvements and are referred to as Improved Los Angeles class boats or 688Is. As of the end of FY2013, 21 of the 62 boats in the class had been retired.

---

[5] For an account of certain U.S. submarine surveillance and intelligence-collection operations during the Cold War, see Sherry Sontag and Christopher Drew with Annette Lawrence Drew, *Blind Man's Bluff* (New York: Public Affairs, 1998).

[6] For additional information on Navy force-level goals, see CRS Report RL32665, *Navy Force Structure and Shipbuilding Plans: Background and Issues for Congress*, by Ronald O'Rourke.

The Seawolf class was originally intended to include about 30 boats, but Seawolf-class procurement was stopped after three boats as a result of the end of the Cold War and associated changes in military requirements. The three Seawolf-class submarines are the *Seawolf* (SSN-21), the *Connecticut* (SSN-22), and the *Jimmy Carter* (SSN-23). SSN-21 and SSN-22 were procured in FY1989 and FY1991 and entered service in 1997 and 1998, respectively. SSN-23 was originally procured in FY1992. Its procurement was suspended in 1992 and then reinstated in FY1996. It entered service in 2005. Seawolf-class submarines are larger than Los Angeles-class boats or previous U.S. Navy SSNs.[7] They are equipped with eight 30-inch-diameter torpedo tubes and can carry a total of 50 torpedoes or cruise missiles. SSN-23 was built to a lengthened configuration compared to the other two ships in the class.[8]

Virginia (SSN-774) Class Program

General

The Virginia-class attack submarine (see **Figure 1**) was designed to be less expensive and better optimized for post-Cold War submarine missions than the Seawolf-class design. The Virginia-class design is slightly larger than the Los Angeles-class design,[9] but incorporates newer technologies. Virginia-class boats currently cost about $2.7 billion each to procure. The first Virginia-class boat entered service in October 2004.

---

[7] Los Angeles-class boats have a beam (i.e., diameter) of 33 feet and a submerged displacement of about 7,150 tons. Seawolf-class boats have a beam of 40 feet. SSN-21 and SSN-22 have a submerged displacement of about 9,150 tons.

[8] SSN-23 is 100 feet longer than SSN-21 and SSN-22 and has a submerged displacement of 12,158 tons.

[9] Virginia-class boats have a beam of 34 feet and a submerged displacement of 7,800 tons.

Figure 1. Virginia-Class Attack Submarine

Source: U.S. Navy file photo accessed by CRS on January 11, 2011, at http://www.navy.mil/search/display.asp? story_id=55715.

Past and Projected Annual Procurement Quantities

Table 1 shows annual numbers of Virginia-class boats procured from FY1998 (the lead boat) through FY2013, and numbers scheduled for procurement under the FY2014-FY2018 Future Years Defense Plan (FYDP).

Table 1. Annual Numbers of Virginia-Class Boats Procured

FY98	FY99	FY00	FY01	FY02	FY03	FY04	FY05	FY06	FY07	FY08
1	1	0	1	1	1	1	1	1	1	1

FY09	FY10	FY11	FY12	FY13	FY14	FY15	FY16	FY17	FY18
1	1	2	2	2	2	2	2	2	2

Source: Table prepared by CRS based on U.S. Navy data.

Multiyear Procurement (MYP)

The 10 Virginia-class boats shown in **Table 1** for the period FY2014-FY2018 are to be procured under a multiyear procurement (MYP) contract[10] that was approved by Congress as part of its

---

[10] For a discussion of MYP contracting, see CRS Report R41909, *Multiyear Procurement (MYP) and Block Buy Contracting in Defense Acquisition: Background and Issues for Congress*, by Ronald O'Rourke and Moshe Schwartz.

action on the FY2013 budget. The eight Virginia-class boats procured in FY2009-FY2013 were procured under a previous MYP contract, and the five Virginia-class boats procured in FY2004-FY2008 were procured under a still-earlier MYP contract. The four boats procured in FY1998-FY2002 were procured under a block buy contract, which is an arrangement somewhat similar to an MYP contract.[11] The boat procured in FY2003 fell between the FY1998-FY2002 block buy contract and the FY2004-FY2008 MYP arrangement, and was contracted for separately.

Joint Production Arrangement

Virginia-class boats are built jointly by General Dynamics' Electric Boat Division (GD/EB) of Groton, CT, and Quonset Point, RI, and Newport News Shipbuilding (NNS), of Newport News, VA, which forms part of Huntington Ingalls Industries (HII).[12] Under the arrangement, GD/EB builds certain parts of each boat, NNS builds certain other parts of each boat, and the yards take turns building the reactor compartments and performing final assembly of the boats. GD/EB is building the reactor compartments and performing final assembly on boats 1, 3, and so on, while NNS is doing so on boats 2, 4, and so on. The arrangement results in a roughly 50-50 division of Virginia-class profits between the two yards and preserves both yards' ability to build submarine reactor compartments (a key capability for a submarine-construction yard) and perform submarine final-assembly work.

The joint production arrangement is a departure from past U.S. submarine construction practices, under which complete submarines were built in individual yards. The joint production arrangement is the product of a debate over the Virginia-class acquisition strategy within Congress, and between Congress and the Department of Defense (DOD), that occurred in 1995-1997 (i.e., during the markup of the FY1996-FY1998 defense budgets). The goal of the arrangement is to keep both GD/EB and NNS involved in building nuclear-powered submarines, and thereby maintain two U.S. shipyards capable of building nuclear-powered submarines, while minimizing the cost penalties of using two yards rather than one to build a submarine design that is being procured at a relatively low annual rate.

Cost-Reduction Effort

The Navy states that it achieved a goal of reducing the procurement cost of Virginia-class submarines so that two boats could be procured in FY2012 for combined cost of $4.0 billion in constant FY2005 dollars—a goal referred to as "2 for 4 in 12." Achieving this goal involved removing about $400 million (in constant FY2005 dollars) from the cost of each submarine. (The Navy calculates that the unit target cost of $2.0 billion in constant FY2005 dollars for each submarine translates into about $2.6 billion for a boat procured in FY2012.)

The Navy says that, in constant FY2005 dollars, about $200 million of the $400 million in the sought-after cost reductions was accomplished simply through the improved economies of scale (e.g., better spreading of shipyard fixed costs and improved learning rates) of producing two submarines per year rather than one per year. The remaining $200 million in sought-after cost

---

[11] For a discussion of block buy contracting, see CRS Report R41909, *Multiyear Procurement (MYP) and Block Buy Contracting in Defense Acquisition: Background and Issues for Congress*, by Ronald O'Rourke and Moshe Schwartz.

[12] GD/EB and NNS are the only two shipyards in the country capable of building nuclear-powered ships. GD/EB builds submarines only, while NNS also builds nuclear-powered aircraft carriers and is capable of building other types of surface ships.

reductions, the Navy says, was accomplished through changes in the ship's design (which will contribute roughly $100 million toward the cost-reduction goal) and changes in the shipyard production process (which will contribute the remaining $100 million or so toward the goal). Some of the design changes are being introduced to Virginia-class boats procured prior to FY2012, but the Navy said the full set of design changes would not be ready for implementation until the FY2012 procurement.

Changes in the shipyard production process are aimed in large part at reducing the total shipyard construction time of a Virginia-class submarine from 72 months to 60 months. (If the ship spends less total time in the shipyard being built, its construction cost will incorporate a smaller amount of shipyard fixed overhead costs.) The principal change involved in reducing shipyard construction time to 60 months involves increasing the size of the modules that form each submarine, so that each submarine can be built out of a smaller number of modules.[13]

Virginia Payload Module (VPM)

DOD and the Navy are considering building Virginia-class boats procured in FY2019 and subsequent years (i.e., the group, or block, of boats that follows the group to be procured under the FY2014-FY2018 MYP contract) with an additional mid-body section, called the Virginia Payload Module (VPM). The VPM, reportedly about 70 feet in length[14] (earlier design concepts for the VPM were reportedly about 94 feet in length),[15] contains four large-diameter, vertical launch tubes that would be used to store and fire additional Tomahawk cruise missiles or other payloads, such as large-diameter unmanned underwater vehicles (UUVs).[16]

The four additional launch tubes in the VPM could carry a total of 28 additional Tomahawk cruise missiles (7 per tube),[17] which would increase the total number of torpedo-sized weapons (such as Tomahawks) carried by the Virginia class design from about 37 to about 65—an increase of about 76%.[18]

Building Virginia-class boats with the VPM would compensate for a sharp loss in submarine force weapon-carrying capacity that will occur with the retirement in FY2026-FY2028 of the Navy's four Ohio-class cruise missile/special operations forces support submarines (SSGNs).[19] Each SSGN is equipped with 24 large-diameter vertical launch tubes, of which 22 can be used to carry up to 7 Tomahawks each, for a maximum of 154 vertically launched Tomahawks per boat,

---

[13] For detailed discussions of the Virginia-class cost-reduction effort, see David C. Johnson et al., "Managing Change on Complex Programs: VIRGINIA Class Cost Reduction," *Naval Engineers Journal*, No. 4, 2009: 79-94; and John D. Butler, "The Sweet Smell of Acquisition Success," *U.S. Naval Institute Proceedings*, June 2011: 22-28.

[14] "Navy Selects Virginia Payload Module Design Concept," *USNI News (*http://news.usni.org*)*, November 4, 2013.

[15] Christopher P. Cavas, "Innovations, No-Shows At Sea-Air-Space Exhibition," *Defense News*, April 18, 2011: 4. See also Christopher P. Cavas, "U.S. Navy Eyes Dual-Mission Sub," *Defense News*, October 17, 2011; and Lee Hudson, "New Virginia-Class Payload Module May Replace SSGN Capability," *Inside the Navy*, October 24, 2011.

[16] For an illustration of the VPM, see http://www.gdeb.com/news/advertising/images/VPM_ad/VPM.pdf, which was accessed by CRS on March 1, 2012.

[17] Michael J. Conner, "Investing in the Undersea Future," *U.S. Naval Institute Proceedings*, June 2011: 16-20.

[18] A Virginia-class SSN can carry about 25 Tomahawks or other torpedo-sized weapons in its four horizontal torpedo tubes and associated torpedo room, and an additional 12 Tomahawk cruise missiles in its bow-mounted vertical lunch tubes, for a total of about 37 torpedo-sized weapons. Another 28 Tomahawks in four mid-body vertical tubes would increase that total by about 76%.

[19] Michael J. Conner, "Investing in the Undersea Future," *U.S. Naval Institute Proceedings*, June 2011: 16-20.

---

or 616 vertically launched Tomahawks for the four boats. Twenty-two Virginia-class boats built with VPMs could carry 616 Tomahawks in their VPMs.

The Navy estimates that adding the VPM would increase the procurement cost of the Virginia-class design by $350 million in current dollars, or by about 13%.[20]

Although funding for the development of the VPM has been reduced in the Navy's proposed FY2014 budget, Secretary of the Navy Ray Mabus testified to the House Armed Services Committee on April 16, 2013, that "with the funding stream that we have going forward, we will have the—we will be where we need to be to make the decision in terms of putting the Virginia payload module into—to that block of submarines [i.e., those procured starting in FY2019]."[21]

FY2014 Funding Request

The Navy's proposed FY2014 budget requested funding for the procurement of two Virginia-class boats. These are to be the first two boats in the 10-boat Virginia-class MYP contract for FY2014-FY2018. The Navy's FY2013 budget submission had projected one Virginia-class boat in FY2014. Congress, as part of its action on the FY2013 DOD budget, added advance procurement (AP) funding in FY2013 to support the procurement of a second Virginia-class boat in FY2014. The Navy's inclusion of a second Virginia-class boat in FY2014 (which increases from 9 to 10 the number of boats in the FY2014-FY2018 MYP contract) follows through on this congressional action.

The Navy's proposed FY2014 budget estimated the combined procurement cost of the two boats at $5,414.2 million. The two boats have received a total of $1,530.8 million in prior-year advance procurement (AP) funding (although this figure may be reduced by the March 1, 2013, sequester), leaving another $3,883.4 million to complete the funding for the two boats.

The Navy's proposed FY2014 budget requested $5,285.3 million in procurement and AP funding for the Virginia class program. This figure includes:

- $2,930.7 million in procurement funding to complete the procurement cost of the first boat requested for FY2014, and to pay part of the procurement cost of the second boat requested for FY2014;

- $1,612.0 million in AP funding for Virginia-class boats to be procured in future fiscal years; and

---

[20] Lee Hudson, "Virginia Payload Module Cost Estimate Down To $350 Million Apiece," *Inside the Navy*, July 22, 2013. Previously, the Navy had testified that adding the VPM would increase the procurement cost of the Virginia-class design by $360 million to $380 million in current dollars. (Source: Spoken testimony of Sean Stackley, the Assistant Secretary of the Navy for Research, Development, and Acquisition [i.e., the Navy's acquisition executive], at a May 8, 2013, hearing on Navy shipbuilding programs before the Seapower subcommittee of the Senate Armed Services Committee, as shown in the transcript for the hearing. See also Olga Belogolova, "Navy Officials Lay Out Fragility Of Shipbuilding Budget To Congress," *Inside the Navy*, May 10, 2013.) Prior to that, the Navy reportedly had estimated that adding the VPM would increase the procurement cost of the Virginia-class design by $400 million to $500 million. (Christopher P. Cavas, "U.S. Navy Eyes Dual-Mission Sub," *Defense News*, October 17, 2011; see also Michael J. Conner, "Investing in the Undersea Future," *U.S. Naval Institute Proceedings*, June 2011: 16-20.)

[21] Transcript of hearing. The transcript does not indicate which Navy official made the comment, but a press report (Jason Sherman, "Navy: Steep Cuts In FY-14 Won't Derail Virginia Payload Module Program," *Inside the Navy*, April 19, 2013) indicates that it was Secretary Mabus.

- $742.6 million in AP funding for Economic Order Quantity (EOQ) purchases (i.e., batch orders) of selected components of the 10 Virginia-class boats to be procured under the FY2014-FY2018 MYP contract. EOQ purchases are a regular feature of the first year or two or an MYP contract.

The Navy proposed to defer to FY2015 the remaining $952.7 million of the procurement cost of the second boat requested for FY2014. This would divide the procurement funding for the boat between two fiscal years (FY2014 and FY2015)—a funding profile sometimes called split funding. In recent instances where split funding has been used to fund Navy ships, the funding has been appropriated using a funding method called incremental funding, under which Congress takes a positive action to approve each of the two annual funding increments. For the second Virginia-class boat requested for FY2014, however, the Navy proposed using a different funding method called advance appropriations, which is a form of full funding that resembles a legislatively locked in form of incremental funding. Under advance appropriations (which is not to be confused with advance procurement [AP] funding), the FY2015 funding increment for the boat would be locked in (i.e., it would be automatic), and Congress would need to take action to stop that increment from being appropriated. Although the Navy in recent years has occasionally expressed interest in using advance appropriations for funding ships, there is little precedent in recent years for funding Navy ships with advance appropriations.

Submarine Construction Industrial Base

In addition to GD/EB and NNS, the submarine construction industrial base includes scores of supplier firms, as well as laboratories and research facilities, in numerous states. Much of the total material procured from supplier firms for the construction of submarines comes from single or sole source suppliers. Observers in recent years have expressed concern for the continued survival of many of these firms. For nuclear-propulsion component suppliers, an additional source of stabilizing work is the Navy's nuclear-powered aircraft carrier construction program.[22] In terms of work provided to these firms, a carrier nuclear propulsion plant is roughly equivalent to five submarine propulsion plants.

Much of the design and engineering portion of the submarine construction industrial base is resident at GD/EB. Smaller portions are resident at NNS and some of the component makers. Several years ago, some observers expressed concern about the Navy's plans for sustaining the design and engineering portion of the submarine construction industrial base. These concerns appear to have receded, in large part because of the Navy's plan to design and procure a next-generation ballistic missile submarine called the Ohio Replacement Program or SSBN(X).[23]

---

[22] For more on this program, see CRS Report RS20643, *Navy Ford (CVN-78) Class Aircraft Carrier Program: Background and Issues for Congress*, by Ronald O'Rourke.

[23] For more on the SBN(X) program, see CRS Report R41129, *Navy Ohio Replacement (SSBN[X]) Ballistic Missile Submarine Program: Background and Issues for Congress*, by Ronald O'Rourke.

Projected SSN Shortfall

Size and Timing of Shortfall

The Navy's FY2014 30-year SSN procurement plan, if implemented, would not be sufficient to maintain a force of 48 SSNs consistently over the long run. As shown in **Table 2**, the Navy projects under the plan that the SSN force would fall below 48 boats starting in FY2025, reach a minimum of 42 boats in FY2029, and remain below 48 boats through 2034. Since the Navy plans to retire the four SSGNs by 2028 without procuring any replacements for them, no SSGNs would be available in 2028 and subsequent years to help compensate for a drop in SSN force level below 48 boats.

The projected SSN shortfall has been discussed in CRS reports and testimony since 1995.

Table 2. Projected SSN Shortfall

As shown in Navy's FY2014 30-Year (FY2014-FY2043) Shipbuilding Plan

Fiscal year	Annual procurement quantity	Projected number of SSNs	Shortfall relative to 48-boat goal	
			Number of ships	**Percent**
14	2	55		
15	2	55		
16	2	53		
17	2	50		
18	2	52		
19	2	52		
20	2	49		
21	2	49		
22	2	48		
23	2	48		
24	1	48		
25	2	47	-1	-2%
26	1	46	-2	-4%
27	2	45	-3	-6%
28	1	43	-5	-10%
29	1	42	-6	-12%
30	1	43	-5	-10%
31	2	44	-4	-8%
32	1	45	-3	-6%
33	1	46	-2	-4%
34	1	47	-1	-2%
35	1	48		
36	1	50		
37	2	51		
38	2	50		
39	1	50		
40	2	50		
41	1	49		
42	2	51		
43	1	51		

Source: Table prepared by CRS based on Navy's FY2014 30-year shipbuilding plan. Percent figures rounded to nearest percent.

2006 Navy Study on Options for Mitigating Projected Shortfall

The Navy in 2006 initiated a study on options for mitigating the projected SSN shortfall. The study was completed in early 2007 and briefed to CRS and the Congressional Budget Office (CBO) on May 22, 2007.[24] At the time of the study, the SSN force was projected to bottom out at 40 boats and then recover to 48 boats by the early 2030s. Principal points in the Navy study (which cite SSN force-level projections as understood at that time) include the following:

- The day-to-day requirement for deployed SSNs is 10.0, meaning that, on average, a total of 10 SSNs are to be deployed on a day-to-day basis.[25]

- The peak projected wartime demand is about 35 SSNs deployed within a certain amount of time. This figure includes both the 10.0 SSNs that are to be deployed on a day-to-day basis and 25 additional SSNs surged from the United States within a certain amount of time.[26]

- Reducing Virginia-class shipyard construction time to 60 months—something that the Navy already plans to do as part of its strategy for meeting the Virginia-class cost-reduction goal (see earlier discussion on cost-reduction goal)—will increase the size of the SSN force by two boats, so that the force would bottom out at 42 boats rather than 40.[27]

- If, in addition to reducing Virginia-class shipyard construction time to 60 months, the Navy also lengthens the service lives of 16 existing SSNs by periods ranging from 3 months to 24 months (with many falling in the range of 9 to 15 months), this would increase the size of the SSN force by another two boats, so that the force would bottom out at 44 boats rather than 40 boats.[28] The total cost of extending the lives of the 16 boats would be roughly $500 million in constant FY2005 dollars.[29]

---

[24] Navy briefing entitled, "SSN Force Structure, 2020-2033," presented to CRS and CBO on May 22, 2007.

[25] The requirement for 10.0 deployed SSNs, the Navy stated in the briefing, was the current requirement at the time the study was conducted.

[26] The peak projected wartime demand of about 35 SSNs deployed within a certain amount of time, the Navy stated, is an internal Navy figure that reflects several studies of potential wartime requirements for SSNs. The Navy stated that these other studies calculated various figures for the number of SSNs that would be required, and that the figure of 35 SSNs deployed within a certain amount of time was chosen because it was representative of the results of these other studies.

[27] If shipyard construction time is reduced from 72 months to 60 months, the result would be a one-year acceleration in the delivery of all boats procured on or after a certain date. In a program in which boats are being procured at a rate of two per year, accelerating by one year the deliveries of all boats procured on or after a certain date will produce a one-time benefit of a single year in which four boats will be delivered to the Navy, rather than two. In the case of the Virginia-class program, this year might be around 2017. As mentioned earlier in the discussion of the Virginia-class cost-reduction goal, the Navy believes that the goal of reducing Virginia-class shipyard construction time is a medium-risk goal. If it turns out that shipyard construction time is reduced to 66 months rather than 60 months (i.e., is reduced by 6 months rather than 12 months), the size of the SSN force would increase by one boat rather than two, and the force would bottom out at 41 boats rather than 42.

[28] The Navy study identified 19 existing SSNs whose service lives currently appear to be extendable by periods of 1 to 24 months. The previous option of reducing Virginia-class shipyard construction time to 60 months, the Navy concluded, would make moot the option of extending the service lives of the three oldest boats in this group of 19, leaving 16 whose service lives would be considered for extension.

[29] The Navy stated that the rough, order-of-magnitude (ROM) cost of extending the lives of 19 SSNs would be $595 million in constant FY2005 dollars, and that the cost of extending the lives of 16 SSNs would be roughly proportional.

- The resulting force that bottoms out at 44 boats could meet the 10.0 requirement for day-to-day deployed SSNs throughout the 2020-2033 period if, as an additional option, about 40 SSN deployments occurring in the eight-year period 2025-2032 were lengthened from six months to seven months. These 40 or so lengthened deployments would represent about one-quarter of all the SSN deployments that would take place during the eight-year period.

- The resulting force that bottoms out at 44 boats could not meet the peak projected wartime demand of about 35 SSNs deployed within a certain amount of time. The force could generate a total deployment of 32 SSNs within the time in question—3 boats (or about 8.6%) less than the 35-boat figure. Lengthening SSN deployments from six months to seven months would not improve the force's ability to meet the peak projected wartime demand of about 35 SSNs deployed within a certain amount of time.

- To meet the 35-boat figure, an additional four SSNs beyond those planned by the Navy would need to be procured. Procuring four additional SSNs would permit the resulting 48-boat force to surge an additional three SSNs within the time in question, so that the force could meet the peak projected wartime demand of about 35 SSNs deployed within a certain amount of time.

- Procuring one to four additional SSNs could also reduce the number of seven-month deployments that would be required to meet the 10.0 requirement for day-to-day deployed SSNs during the period 2025-2032. Procuring one additional SSN would reduce the number of seven-month deployments during this period to about 29; procuring two additional SSNs would reduce it to about 17, procuring three additional SSNs would reduce it to about 7, and procuring four additional SSNs would reduce it to 2.

The Navy added a number of caveats to these results, including but not limited to the following:

- The requirement for 10.0 SSNs deployed on a day-to-day basis is a current requirement that could change in the future.

- The peak projected wartime demand of about 35 SSNs deployed within a certain amount of time is an internal Navy figure that reflects recent analyses of potential future wartime requirements for SSNs. Subsequent analyses of this issue could result in a different figure.

- The identification of 19 SSNs as candidates for service life extension reflects current evaluations of the material condition of these boats and projected use rates for their nuclear fuel cores. If the material condition of these boats years from now turns out to be worse than the Navy currently projects, some of them might no longer be suitable for service life extension. In addition, if world conditions over the next several years require these submarines to use up their nuclear fuel cores more quickly than the Navy now projects, then the amounts of time that their service lives might be extended could be reduced partially, to zero, or to less than zero (i.e., the service lives of the boats, rather than being extended, might need to be shortened).

- The analysis does not take into account potential rare events, such as accidents, that might force the removal an SSN from service before the end of its expected service life.[30]

- Seven-month deployments might affect retention rates for submarine personnel.

Issues for Congress

Impact of March 1, 2013, Sequester on FY2013 Funding

One issue for Congress concerns the impact on the Virginia-class program of the March 1, 2013, sequester on FY2013 funding (and unobligated prior-year funding) for the Virginia-class program. DOD's June 2013 report to Congress on the March 1, 2013, sequester states that the sequester reduced FY2013 and prior-year procurement funding for the Virginia-class program by $492.3 million.[31] A June 14, 2013, press report states:

> Sequestration may make it impossible to buy 10 Virginia-class attack submarines in the coming years as part of a multiyear contract despite two House committees voting to provide enough money for the ships, Navy Secretary Ray Mabus told reporters last week....
>
> Mabus said at a Defense Writers Group breakfast on June 13 that buying 10 subs for essentially the price of nine is clearly a good thing, but "because of sequestration, it makes it very difficult to get that 10th boat in."[32]

Funding Method for 2nd Boat in FY2014

Another issue for Congress is whether the second of the two Virginia-class boats requested for procurement in FY2014 should be funded using traditional (i.e., single-year) full funding, incremental funding, or (as the Navy proposes) advance appropriations.

Under *traditional (i.e., single-year) full funding*, an end item (in this case, a ship) is fully funded in the year of its procurement, and none of its procurement cost is deferred to a subsequent year. DOD's full funding policy requires the use of traditional full funding as the default funding method for end items acquired through the procurement title of the annual DOD appropriations act. As a consequence, traditional full funding is used for funding most DOD procurement end items, including most Navy ships.

---

[30] In January 2005, the Los Angeles-class SSN San Francisco (SSN-711) was significantly damaged in a collision with an undersea mountain near Guam. The ship was repaired in part by transplanting onto it the bow section of the deactivated sister ship Honolulu (SSN-718). (See, for example, Associated Press, "Damaged Submarine To Get Nose Transplant," *Seattle Post-Intelligencer*, June 26, 2006.) Prior to the decision to repair the San Francisco, the Navy considered the option of removing it from service. (See, for example, William H. McMichael, "Sub May Not Be Worth Saving, Analyst Says," *Navy Times*, February 28, 2005; Gene Park, "Sub Repair Bill: $11M," *Pacific Sunday News (Guam)*, May 8, 2005.)

[31] *Department of Defense Report on the Joint Committee Sequestration for Fiscal Year 2013*, June 2013, p. 36A (pdf page 86 of 438).

[32] Megan Eckstein, "Sequestration May Put 10th Virginia Sub At Risk Despite House Funding," *Inside the Navy*, June 17, 2013.

Under *incremental funding*, an end item's procurement cost (or, more precisely, the portion of its procurement cost that has not already been paid for through advance procurement [AP] funding provided in one or more years prior to the item's year of procurement) is divided between its year of procurement and one or more subsequent years, and Congress needs to take a positive action to appropriate each annual funding increment. Dividing an end item's procurement funding between two fiscal years (the item's year of procurement and the following year) is sometimes called split funding. It has become standard practice in recent years to fund the procurement of amphibious assault ships (large amphibious ships, designed LHA or LHD in Navy parlance, that look like medium-sized aircraft carriers) using two-year incremental funding, and to fund the procurement of aircraft carriers with incremental funding stretching across multiple years. (Current authority granted by Congress permits the Navy to use six-year incremental funding for aircraft carriers, meaning that an aircraft carrier's procurement cost can be divided between the ship's year of procurement and the next five years).

Under *advance appropriations*, an end item's procurement cost (or, again more precisely, the portion of its procurement cost that has not already been paid for through advance procurement [AP] funding provided in one or more years prior to the item's year of procurement) is divided between its year of procurement and one or more subsequent years, as would be the case under incremental funding. Unlike incremental funding, however, the funding increments in the years after the year of procurement are legislatively locked into place (i.e., they would be "automatic"), and Congress would need to take action to stop those increments from being appropriated. Under DOD's funding regulations, advance appropriations qualifies as an alternative form of full funding (an alternative, that is, to traditional [i.e., single-year] full funding), and can be understood as a legislatively locked in form of incremental funding. Although the Navy in recent years has occasionally expressed interest in using advance appropriations for funding ships, there is little precedent in recent years for funding Navy ships with advance appropriations.

Detailed discussions of the policy considerations pertaining to the use of traditional full funding, incremental funding, and advance appropriations in procuring DOD procurement end items, particularly Navy ships, can be found in two other CRS reports.[33] In general, however, supporters of using each of these funding methods for the second Virginia-class boat in FY2014 might make arguments along the lines outlined below.

Supporters of using traditional (i.e., single-year) full funding might argue the following:

- DOD's full funding policy was imposed on DOD by Congress many years ago, and is intended to strengthen DOD budgeting discipline and facilitate effective congressional oversight of DOD procurement costs. There is little precedent for using incremental funding for ships other than aircraft carriers and amphibious assault ships, and little precedent for using advance appropriations for funding the procurement of ships of any kind. Using incremental funding or advance appropriations to fund the second Virginia-class boat in FY2014 would set a precedent that could lead to more widespread use of something other than traditional (i.e., single-year) full funding for Navy ships other than aircraft carriers and amphibious assault ships, which could weaken adherence to DOD's full funding policy.

---

[33] See CRS Report RL31404, *Defense Procurement: Full Funding Policy—Background, Issues, and Options for Congress*, by Ronald O'Rourke and Stephen Daggett, and CRS Report RL32776, *Navy Ship Procurement: Alternative Funding Approaches—Background and Options for Congress*, by Ronald O'Rourke.

- A principal rationale for making an exception to DOD's full funding policy and permitting the use of incremental funding for aircraft carriers and amphibious assault ships is that since these are very expensive ships that are procured once every few years, fully funding them in a single year would cause a spike in Navy funding requirements that, in a situation of a fixed Navy budget top line, could require funding for other Navy or DOD programs to be shifted to earlier or later fiscal years, causing potentially expensive disruptions in those other programs. Using incremental funding for aircraft carriers and amphibious assault ships mitigates these budget spikes by spreading the procurement costs of these ships over two or more years, reducing the need for offsetting and potentially expensive disruptions to the funding streams of other programs. In the case of the Virginia-class submarine program, the rationale of mitigating a once-every-few-years budget spike does not apply, because Virginia-class submarines are procured every year.

- Both Congress (through its decision to provide advance procurement funding in FY2013 for a second Virginia-class boat in FY2014) and the Administration (through its inclusion of a second Virginia-class boat in its proposed FY2014 Navy budget) have signaled support for procuring a second Virginia-class boat in FY2014. Given this support for procuring the boat in FY2014, policymakers should be willing to make the necessary sacrifices to funding for other DOD programs in FY2014 to accommodate the full funding of this boat in FY2014.

Supporters of using incremental funding might argue the following:

- Although incremental funding normally is used only for aircraft carriers and amphibious assault ships, it has occasionally been used for other types of ships as well. All three Zumwalt (DDG-1000) class destroyers were funded with two-year incremental funding in FY2007 and FY2009,[34] and SSN-23, the third and final Seawolf (SSN-21) class attack submarine, had its funding completed with a series of funding increments in FY1996-FY1998.[35] There is thus precedent for occasionally incrementally funding ships other than aircraft carriers when policymakers deem it necessary.

- Navy officials stated in 2012 that FY2014 is a particularly tight budget year for the Navy, and that this is why the Navy's FY2013 budget submission projected only one Virginia-class boat in FY2014. FY2014 remains a tight budget year for the Navy, particularly given the March 1, 2013, sequester on DOD funding. In this context, incrementally funding the second Virginia-class boat requested for FY2014 could be of particular help to the Navy for avoiding potentially expensive disruptions to the funding streams for other Navy programs in FY2014.

- One of the principal arguments for avoiding use of incremental funding—that it ties the hands of future Congresses by creating a need for those Congresses to complete the funding of procurement end items that were partially funded by a

---

[34] The first two Zumwalt-class ships were procured in FY2007 using two-year incremental funding in FY2007 and FY2008; the third was procured in FY2009 using two-year incremental funding in FY2009 and FY2010.

[35] For the case of SSN-23, see CRS Report RL32776, *Navy Ship Procurement: Alternative Funding Approaches—Background and Options for Congress*, by Ronald O'Rourke.

previous Congress—does not apply in the case of two-year incremental funding for this boat, because the second increment of funding will occur in the FY2015, which will be acted on by the current Congress, and because, more generally, the decision to tie the hands of future Congresses has already been made by Congress's decision, as part of its action on the FY2013 budget, to approve an MYP contract that strongly commits future Congresses to the procurement of Virginia-class boats through FY2018.

Supporters of using advance appropriations might argue the following:

- Navy officials stated in 2012 that FY2014 is a particularly tight budget year for the Navy, and that this is why the Navy's FY2013 budget submission projected only one Virginia-class boat in FY2014. FY2014 remains a tight budget year for the Navy, particularly given the March 1, 2013, sequester on DOD funding. In this context, using advance appropriations to fund the second Virginia-class boat requested for FY2014 could be of particular help to the Navy for avoiding potentially expensive disruptions to the funding streams for other Navy programs in FY2014.

- Although there is little precedent for using advance appropriations for funding the procurement of Navy ships, advance appropriations is recognized under DOD budgeting policy as a form of full funding. In that sense, using advance appropriations to fund the boat would represent less of a departure from DOD's full funding policy than would funding the boat with incremental funding.

- Legislatively locking into place the FY2015 funding increment for the boat, as would happen under advance appropriations, would be consistent in general intent with Congress's decision, as part of its action on the FY2013 budget, to approve an MYP contract that strongly commits future Congresses to the procurement of Virginia-class boats through FY2018.

Virginia-Class Procurement Rate More Generally in Coming Years

Another issue for Congress concerns the Virginia-class procurement rate more generally in coming years, particularly in the context of the SSN shortfall projected for FY2025-FY2034 shown in **Table 2** and the larger debate over future U.S. defense strategy and defense spending.

Mitigating Projected SSN Shortfall

In addition to lengthening SSN deployments to 7 months and extending the service lives of existing SSNs by periods ranging from 3 months to 24 months (see "2006 Navy Study on Options for Mitigating Projected Shortfall" above), options for more fully mitigating the projected SSN shortfall include

- refueling a small number of (perhaps one to five) existing SSNs and extending their service lives by 10 years or more, and

- putting additional Virginia-class boats into the 30-year shipbuilding plan.

It is not clear whether it would be feasible or cost-effective to refuel existing SSNs and extend their service lives by 10 or more years, given factors such as limits on submarine pressure hull life.

Larger Debate on Defense Strategy and Defense Spending

Some observers—particularly those who propose reducing U.S. defense spending as part of an effort to reduce the federal budget deficit—have recommended that the SSN force-level goal be reduced to something less than 48 boats, and/or that Virginia-class procurement be reduced. A June 2010 report from a group called the Sustainable Defense Task Force recommends a Navy of 230 ships, including 37 SSNs,[36] and a September 2010 report from the Cato Institute recommends a Navy of 241 ships, including 40 SSNs.[37] Both reports recommend limiting Virginia-class procurement to one boat per year, as does a September 2010 report from the Center for American Progress.[38] A November 2010 report from a group called the Debt Reduction Task Force recommends "deferring" Virginia-class procurement.[39] The November 2010 draft recommendations of the co-chairs of the Fiscal Commission include recommendations for reducing procurement of certain weapon systems; the Virginia-class program is not among them.

Other observers have recommended that the SSN force-level goal should be increased to something higher than 48 boats, particularly in light of Chinese naval modernization.[40] The July 2010 report of an independent panel that assessed the 2010 Quadrennial Defense Review (QDR)—an assessment that is required by the law governing QDRs (10 U.S.C. 118)—recommends a Navy of 346 ships, including 55 SSNs.[41] An April 2010 report from the Heritage Foundation recommends a Navy of 309 ships, including 55 SSNs.[42]

Factors to consider in assessing whether to maintain, increase, or reduce the SSN force-level goal and/or planned Virginia-class procurement include but are not limited to the federal budget and debt situation, the value of SSNs in defending U.S. interests and implementing U.S. national security strategy, and potential effects on the submarine industrial base.

As discussed earlier, Virginia-class boats scheduled for procurement in FY2014 are to be covered under an MYP contract for the period FY2014-FY2018. This MYP contract is to include the procurement of two Virginia-class boats in FY2014. If this contract is awarded, and fewer than two boats were subsequently procured in FY2014, the Navy might need to terminate the MYP contract and pay a cancellation penalty to the contractor.

---

[36] *Debt, Deficits, and Defense, A Way Forward[:] Report of the Sustainable Defense Task Force*, June 11, 2010, pp. 19-20, 31.

[37] Benjamin H. Friedman and Christopher Preble, *Budgetary Savings from Military Restraint*, Washington, Cato Institute, September 23, 2010 (Policy Analysis No. 667), pp. 9.

[38] Lawrence J. Korb and Laura Conley, *Strong and Sustainable[:] How to Reduce Military Spending While Keeping Our Nation Safe*, Center for American Progress, September 2010, p. 19-20.

[39] Debt Reduction Task Force, *Restoring America's Future[:] Reviving the Economy, Cutting Spending and Debt, and Creating a Simple, Pro-Growth Tax System*, November 2010, p. 103.

[40] For further discussion of China's naval modernization effort, see CRS Report RL33153, *China Naval Modernization: Implications for U.S. Navy Capabilities—Background and Issues for Congress*, by Ronald O'Rourke.

[41] Stephen J. Hadley and William J. Perry, co-chairmen, et al., *The QDR in Perspective: Meeting America's National Security Needs In the 21st Century, The Final Report of the Quadrennial Defense Review Independent Panel*, Washington, 2010, Figure 3-2 on page 58.

[42] A *Strong National Defense[:] The Armed Forces America Needs and What They Will Cost*, Heritage Foundation, April 5, 2011, pp. 25-26.

Program Issues Raised in January 2014 DOT&E Report

Another oversight issue for Congress concerns Virginia-class program issues raised in a January 2014 report from the DOD's Director, Operational Test and Evaluation (DOT&E)—DOT&E's annual report for FY2013. Regarding the Virginia-class program, the report stated:

Assessment

• The October 2013 DOT&E classified report details Virginia's ability to host NSW [Naval Special Warfare] missions from a DDS [Dry Deck Shelter] and concluded the following:

- Virginia class submarines are capable of hosting the DDS system.

- Virginia class submarines can remain covert during NSW missions in some environments against some threat forces. Testing was not sufficient to fully evaluate the covertness of the class during DDS operations against expected threats. DOT&E's report provided estimates for probability to remain covert based on the data available. Furthermore, the Navy's primary metric for assessing success in these missions is a binary probability, which is infeasible to measure.

- Operational testing was adequate for an assessment of the Virginia class submarine's effectiveness and suitability for NSW missions using a DDS only against a low-end threat. The Navy's Commander, Operational Test and Evaluation Force (COTF) did not conduct test execution in accordance with the DOT&E-approved test plan. Specifically, COTF failed to collect positional data from the assigned simulated opposing forces, which limited the ability to assess covertness during these operations. Additionally, the testing did not provide data to address acoustic vulnerabilities during NSW operations using a DDS.

- The Virginia class submarine is suitable for NSW operations using a DDS; however, the Navy identified shortcomings in the Virginia class in testing.

    ▪ Space limitations onboard the submarines restrict movement to and from the control room, which potentially impedes the ship's ability to execute damage control procedures in the event a casualty occurs during NSW operations using a DDS.

    ▪ During conditions of low visibility, including nighttime operations, Special Operations Force (SOF) members on the surface may have difficulty seeing the photonics mast of a submerged submarine, which is used to guide the movement of the SOF as they return to the submarine.

    ▪ The Navy made modifications to the SEAL Delivery Vehicle (SDV) Auxiliary Life Support System (ALSS) used in some DDS operations. These modifications allow for increased air pressure and as a result, more available man-hours to support missions. The Virginia class air supply system to pressurize the ALSS does not support operating at the higher pressures.

• The May 2013 DOT&E report on Virginia's operational capabilities in the Arctic and the Virginia's susceptibility to low-frequency passive acoustic detection concluded that:

- Testing was adequate for an assessment of effectiveness and suitability to support general Arctic operations and of the susceptibility of the submarine to detection by passive acoustic sensors. The Navy conducted the testing in accordance with the DOT&E-approved Test and Evaluation Master Plan and test plan but data were not available to conduct the desired quantitative assessment because the Navy did not retain the data following the testing.

- Virginia class submarines are effective at supporting general operations in the Arctic but remain ineffective at ASW against some targets, which is unchanged from previous testing reported on by DOT&E. During testing, the Virginia class submarine was hampered with a failure of its sonar system's TB-29 towed array. The failure of the towed-array affected the submarine's performance because it provided the longest-range detections of acoustic contacts. However, these arrays are known to be fragile and do frequently fail during operations.

- As part of the operational testing, an evaluation of the Depth-Encoded Ice-Keel Avoidance (IKA) mode of the Acoustic Rapid Commercial Off-the-Shelf Insertion (A-RCI) sonar system was included. Ice-keels extend down from the ice canopy above the submarine when operating in regions of the Arctic covered by ice. This Depth-Encoded IKA mode uses active sonar with the intention of providing operators with location, size, and depth of ice-keels so that the submarine can avoid colliding with them. The testing showed that the Depth-Encoded IKA is fundamentally limited by the precision to which a submarine can know the propagation path of the active sonar and as a result, the Depth-Encoded IKA is unable to achieve the threshold for accuracy established by the Navy.

- Virginia class submarines are difficult to detect with low-frequency passive acoustic sensors. Like all other classes of U.S. submarines, when operating at high speeds Virginia class submarines become more susceptible to detection by passive acoustic sensors.

- Virginia class submarines provide less Arctic capability than the Seawolf and improved Los Angeles class submarines. Some regions of the Arctic are characterized by tight vertical clearances between the shallow ocean floor below and the thick ice canopy above. Virginia lacks a hardened sail, and is therefore limited in the thickness of ice through which the submarine can safely surface.

- The Virginia class submarine is operationally suitable for supporting general Arctic operations but suffers from some reliability shortcomings:

  • The IKA modes of the A-RCI sonar system reliability require improvement to support extended periods of challenging under-ice operations. After a decade of development and fielding, no hardware or software variant of A-RCI has come close to the Navy's reliability requirement, which is based on an operational need. More reliable sonar processing hardware is typically brought onboard because of the poor A-RCI reliability.

  • The common methods of removing carbon dioxide and hydrogen waste gas consistently failed during operations in the cold Arctic environment.

  • The handling system for the Virginia class submarine's Buoyant Cable Antenna, used for communications during operations under the ice canopy, is susceptible to freezing preventing subsequent deployment or retrieval.

  • The Virginia class submarine suffers from excessive condensation in the cold Arctic environment. In general, this is an insulation problem since water vapor will condense on any surface with a temperature below the local dew point. Excessive condensation has the potential to cause problems with electronic systems.

• DOT&E's classified report on Virginia's modernization FOT&E, issued in November 2012, concluded the following:

- Virginia's operational effectiveness is dependent on the mission conducted. The modernization of the sonar and fire control systems (A-RCI and AN/BYG-1) with the APB

09 software did not change (improve or degrade) the performance of the Virginia class for the missions tested. DOT&E's assessment of mission effectiveness remains the same for ASW; Intelligence, Surveillance, and Reconnaissance; High-Density Contact Management; situational awareness; and Mine Avoidance. DOT&E's overall assessment of Information Assurance remains unchanged from IOT&E, although the new software represents an improvement in Information Assurance over previous systems.

- Although Virginia was not effective for some of the missions tested, it remains an effective replacement for the Los Angeles class submarine, providing similar mission performance and improved covertness.

- Testing to examine ASW-attack and situational awareness in high-density environments was adequate for the system software that was tested but not adequate for the software version that the Navy fielded. After completion of operational testing, the Navy issued software changes intended to address the severe performance problems observed with the Wide Aperture Array. The Navy has not completed operational testing on the new software, which is fielded on deployed submarines. DOT&E assesses that the late fix of the array's deficiencies is a result of the Navy's schedule-driven development processes, which fields new increments without completing adequate developmental testing.

- The Navy collected adequate data to assess the suitability of the sonar and fire control systems. Insufficient data were collected to reassess the suitability of Virginia's hull, mechanical, electrical, or electronic systems; however, these data were not expected to demonstrate significantly different reliability compared to what was observed in IOT&E. Of note, the installation of the new APB 09 on Virginia's A-RCI sonar system will degrade the reliability of the sonar system on these submarines relative to what was demonstrated in the IOT&E.

Recommendations

• Status of Previous Recommendations.

- The Navy has made progress in addressing 23 of the 30 recommendations contained in the November 2009 classified FOT&E report. Of the seven outstanding recommendations, the significant unclassified recommendations are:

1. Test against a diesel submarine threat surrogate in order to evaluate Virginia's capability, detectability, and survivability against modern diesel-electric submarines.

2. Conduct an FOT&E to examine Virginia's susceptibility to airborne ASW threats such as Maritime Patrol Aircraft and helicopters.

- The following recommendations from the FY12 Annual Report remain open and the Navy should work to address them in the upcoming fiscal year:

3. Coordinate the Virginia, A-RCI, and AN/BYG-1 Test and Evaluation Master Plans and utilize Undersea Enterprise Capstone documents to facilitate testing efficiencies.

4. Complete the verification, validation, and accreditation of the TSA method used for Virginia class Block III items.

5. Repeat the FOT&E event to determine Virginia's susceptibility to low-frequency active sonar and the submarine's ability to conduct Anti-Surface Warfare in a low-frequency active environment. This testing should include a Los Angeles class submarine operating in the same environment to enable comparison with the Virginia class.

• FY13 Recommendations. The Virginia DDS and Arctic reports generated 16 recommendations. The following are unclassified recommendations listed in the October 2013 FOT&E report. The Navy should:

1. Reconsider the metrics used to assess Virginia class submarine's ability to covertly conduct mass swimmer lockout operations using the DDS.

2. Evaluate the possible acoustic vulnerabilities associated with SDV employment.

3. Seek additional evaluations of Virginia class operations with a DDS to improve understanding of deployment time for operations and operationally evaluate covertness.

4. Confirm that the access to and from the Control Room during DDS operations meet the requirements of the Submarine Safety Program for accessibility and are sufficient to provide for adequate damage control in the event of casualties.

5. The Navy should investigate and implement methods to aid the SOF in identifying the submarine during operations in conditions of low visibility.

6. Investigate modifying the reducer in the air charging system to allow higher air pressure for the SDV Auxiliary Life Support System in order to provide increased flexibility for SDV missions that can be hosted from Virginia class submarines.

7. Re-evaluate the accuracy requirements for the IKA sonar modes and investigate the calibration of those modes.

8. Continue the reliability improvement program for the TB-29 towed-array or pursue the development of a new array.

9. Improve the reliability of the A-RCI IKA sonar modes.

10. Modify atmosphere control subsystems to operate properly in the freezing waters of the Arctic Ocean.

11. Modify the handling system of the Buoyant Antenna Cable to prevent its freezing in the cold Arctic environment.

12. Continue to collect data on the susceptibility of the Virginia class to low-frequency passive systems and conduct a more quantitative assessment (e.g., determine detection ranges for different ship postures).[43]

---

[43] Department of Defense, Director, Operational Test and Evaluation, *FY2013 Annual Report*, January 2014, pp. 240-242.

Legislative Activity for FY2014

FY2014 National Defense Authorization Act (H.R. 3304/P.L. 113-66)

House

The House Armed Services Committee, in its report (H.Rept. 113-102 of June 7, 2013) on the FY2014 National Defense Authorization Act (H.R. 1960), recommends increasing by $492 million the Navy's request for FY2014 procurement funding for the Virginia class program, and approving the Navy's request for FY2014 advance procurement (AP) funding for the Virginia class program (page 387). The additional $492 million in procurement funding matches almost exactly the $492.3 million in procurement funding sequestered from the Virginia-class program by the March 1, 2013, sequester.

Senate

The Senate Armed Services Committee, in its report (S.Rept. 113-44 of June 20, 2013) on the FY2014 National Defense Authorization Act (S. 1197), recommends approving the Navy's request for procurement and advance procurement (AP) funding for the Virginia-class program (pages 295-296).

Final Version

The final version of the FY2014 National Defense Authorization Act (H.R. 3304/P.L. 113-66 of December 26, 2013) recommends increasing by $492 million the Navy's request for FY2014 procurement funding for the Virginia class program, and approving the Navy's request for FY2014 advance procurement (AP) funding for the Virginia class program (see pdf page 402 of 532 of the explanatory statement for H.R. 3304). The additional $492 million in procurement funding matches almost exactly the $492.3 million in procurement funding sequestered from the Virginia-class program by the March 1, 2013, sequester.

FY2014 DOD Appropriations Act (Division C of H.R. 3547/P.L. 113-76)

House

The House Appropriations Committee, in its report (H.Rept. 113-113 of June 17, 2013) on the FY2014 DOD Appropriations Act (H.R. 2397), recommends increasing by $950 million the Navy's request for FY2014 procurement funding for the Virginia class program, and approving the Navy's request for FY2014 advance procurement (AP) funding for the Virginia class program, with the additional $950 million in procurement funding to be used to "Fully fund the Virginia class program" (pages 163 and 164). H.Rept. 113-113 states that

> the Navy requested authority to incrementally fund a Virginia Class Submarine in fiscal year 2014. The Congress has authorized and appropriated funding for 18 fully funded Virginia Class Submarines in the years prior to fiscal year 2014. The Committee does not understand

why funding requested for this particular submarine requires violating the Department of Defense's long standing full funding policy. The Committee is puzzled by Navy claims of billions of dollars in savings for the taxpayers as it is the Committee's understanding that these savings come from the fact that the program is conducting a multi-year procurement of ten submarines and not from the fact that one of the submarines is incrementally funded. Quality budget discipline, not funding gimmicks, is called for more than ever in these times of decreasing budgets and budget uncertainty. (Page 165)

Section 8010 of H.R. 2397 as reported by the House Appropriations Committee provides authority for using multiyear procurement (MYP) contracting for certain DOD acquisition programs, including the Virginia class program. (Section 8010 of the FY2013 DOD appropriations act [Division C of H.R. 933/P.L. 113-6 of March 26, 2013] similarly provided authority for using MYP contracting for the Virginia class program.)

Senate

The Senate Appropriations Committee, in its report (S.Rept. 113-85 of August 1, 2013) on FY2014 DOD Appropriations Act (S. 1429), recommends increasing by $227 million the Navy's request for FY2014 procurement funding for the Virginia class program, with the increase being for "Maintain critical industrial base: Virginia class submarine," and approving the Navy's request for FY2014 advance procurement (AP) funding for the Virginia class program (page 100, lines 3, 4, and 20, and page 101, line 20). The $227 million in additional Virginia-class procurement funding is provided in the line item for completion of prior-year shipbuilding (line 20), and is noted in **Section 8072** of S. 1429 as reported by the committee, which concerns funding for this line item.

Section 8010 of S. 1429 as reported by the committee provides authority for using multiyear procurement (MYP) contracting for certain DOD acquisition programs, including the Virginia class program. (Section 8010 of the FY2013 DOD appropriations act [Division C of H.R. 933/P.L. 113-6 of March 26, 2013] similarly provided authority for using MYP contracting for the Virginia class program.)

S.Rept. 113-85 recommends reducing by $59.87 million funding that the Navy had requested for research and development work on the Virginia class, with the reduction being for "Program termination: VA class module program terminated due to affordability." (Page 159, line 112.) The report states:

> *Virginia Payload Module.*—The Fiscal Year 2013 Defense Appropriations Act reduced the fiscal year 2013 budget request for the Virginia Payload Module by $90,000,000. The Committees was concerned with increasing the Virginia-class submarine size by a third to accommodate a 93.7 foot module in the submarine's center. The Committee believes that the module's requirements are not defined, and will result in instability to a proven submarine design, disrupt a stable production line, and add significant cost risk which is not affordable in these difficult fiscal times. Initial cost estimates for development alone were $800,000,000. Since then, the Navy has completed the requirements validation, but the Joint Requirements Oversight Committee validation is still incomplete. The Committee recommends no funding for the Virginia Payload Module in fiscal year 2014. (Page 161)

Final Version

The final version of the FY2014 DOD Appropriations Act (H.R. 3547/P.L. 113-76 of January 17, 2014) increases by $950 million the Navy's request for FY2014 procurement funding for the Virginia class program, with the increase being for "Fully fund the Virginia class submarine program." The act also approves the Navy's request for FY2014 advance procurement (AP) funding for the Virginia class program (see pdf pages 159 and 160 of 351 of the explanatory statement for Division C of H.R. 3547). Of the $960 million in shipbuilding procurement funding provided by the act for the completion of Navy ships procured in prior years, $227 million is for the Virginia-class program; this funding is noted in **Section 8072** of the act, and in the explanatory statement for Division C of H.R. 3547 (see pdf page 160 of 351).

Regarding research and development funding for the Virginia Payload Module (VPM), the explanatory statement states:

VIRGINIA PAYLOAD MODULE

The fiscal year 2014 budget request for the Virginia Payload Module (VPM) is $59,000,000. The agreement fully funds the budget request; however, concerns remain over increasing the Virginia-class submarine size to accommodate a 93.7 foot module in the submarine's center. The module's requirements are not defined, which likely will result in instability to a proven submarine design, disrupt a stable production line, and add significant cost to the current estimates. These concerns are raised due to a history of cost growth on previous submarine development efforts. For instance, in 1999, the Navy began designing the conversion of four SSBN submarines to SSGN configurations with the initial cost estimates for a four-boat program of $2,400,000,000. By the time these submarines were converted, the cost was $4,000,000,000, or an increase of 66 percent above the initial estimates. Similarly, when the Navy modified SSN-23, it increased the submarine's cost by $887,000,000 for a total of $3,300,000,000 for one submarine.

The Department of the Navy recently received Joint Requirements Oversight Committee approval of the capabilities development document for the VPM. The document includes two additional key performance parameters for controlling costs: the non-recurring engineering cost to design the modification is limited to $800,000,000 in constant fiscal year 2010 dollars for development, and the production cost is limited to $475,000,000 for the lead ship and $350,000,000 for the follow-on ships. The Navy is directed not to exceed these cost thresholds.

The Secretary of the Navy shall create a separate budget line item to enable additional congressional oversight and increase transparency into the costs of VPM. Furthermore, the Secretary shall submit a bi-annual report to the congressional defense committees describing the actions the Navy is taking to minimize costs. The agreement fences $20,000,000 until the first bi-annual report is provided to the congressional defense committees. (pdf page 239 of 351)

Appendix A. Past SSN Force-Level Goals

This appendix summarizes attack submarine force-level goals since the Reagan Administration (1981-1989).

The Reagan-era plan for a 600-ship Navy included an objective of achieving and maintaining a force of 100 SSNs.

The George H. W. Bush Administration's proposed Base Force plan of 1991-1992 originally called for a Navy of more than 400 ships, including 80 SSNs.[44] In 1992, however, the SSN goal was reduced to about 55 boats as a result of a 1992 Joint Staff force-level requirement study (updated in 1993) that called for a force of 51 to 67 SSNs, including 10 to 12 with Seawolf-level acoustic quieting, by the year 2012.[45]

The Clinton Administration, as part of its 1993 Bottom-Up Review (BUR) of U.S. defense policy, established a goal of maintaining a Navy of about 346 ships, including 45 to 55 SSNs.[46] The Clinton Administration's 1997 QDR supported a requirement for a Navy of about 305 ships and established a tentative SSN force-level goal of 50 boats, "contingent on a reevaluation of peacetime operational requirements."[47] The Clinton Administration later amended the SSN figure to 55 boats (and therefore a total of about 310 ships).

The reevaluation called for in the 1997 QDR was carried out as part of a Joint Chiefs of Staff (JCS) study on future requirements for SSNs that was completed in December 1999. The study had three main conclusions:

- "that a force structure below 55 SSNs in the 2015 [time frame] and 62 [SSNs] in the 2025 time frame would leave the CINC's [the regional military commanders-in-chief] with insufficient capability to respond to urgent crucial demands without gapping other requirements of higher national interest. Additionally, this force structure [55 SSNs in 2015 and 62 in 2025] would be sufficient to meet the modeled war fighting requirements";

- "that to counter the technologically pacing threat would require 18 Virginia class SSNs in the 2015 time frame"; and

---

[44] For the 80-SSN figure, see Statement of Vice Admiral Roger F. Bacon, U.S. Navy, Assistant Chief of Naval Operations (Undersea Warfare) in U.S. Congress, House Armed Services Committee, Subcommittee on Seapower and Strategic and Critical Materials, *Submarine Programs*, March 20, 1991, pp. 10-11, or Statement of Rear Admiral Raymond G. Jones, Jr., U.S. Navy, Deputy Assistant Chief of Naval Operations (Undersea Warfare), in U.S. Congress, Senate Armed Services Committee, Subcommittee on Projection Forces and Regional Defense, *Submarine Programs*, June 7, 1991, pp. 10-11.

[45] See Richard W. Mies, "Remarks to the NSL Annual Symposium," *Submarine Review*, July 1997, p. 35; "Navy Sub Community Pushes for More Subs than Bottom-Up Review Allowed," *Inside the Navy*, November 7, 1994, pp. 1, 8-9; *Attack Submarines in the Post-Cold War Era: The Issues Facing Policymakers*, op. cit., p. 14; Robert Holzer, "Pentagon Urges Navy to Reduce Attack Sub Fleet to 50," *Defense News*, March 15-21, 1993, p. 10; Barbara Nagy, " Size of Sub Force Next Policy Battle," *New London Day*, July 20, 1992, pp. A1, A8.

[46] Secretary of Defense Les Aspin, U.S. Department of Defense, *Report on the Bottom-Up Review*, October 1993, pp. 55-57.

[47] Secretary of Defense William S. Cohen, U.S. Department of Defense, *Report of the Quadrennial Defense Review*, May 1997, pp. 29, 30, 47.

- "that 68 SSNs in the 2015 [time frame] and 76 [SSNs] in the 2025 time frame would meet all of the CINCs' and national intelligence community's highest operational and collection requirements."[48]

The conclusions of the 1999 JCS study were mentioned in discussions of required SSN force levels, but the figures of 68 and 76 submarines were not translated into official Department of Defense (DOD) force-level goals.

The George W. Bush Administration's report on the 2001 QDR revalidated the amended requirement from the 1997 QDR for a fleet of about 310 ships, including 55 SSNs. In revalidating this and other U.S. military force-structure goals, the report cautioned that as DOD's "transformation effort matures—and as it produces significantly higher output of military value from each element of the force—DOD will explore additional opportunities to restructure and reorganize the Armed Forces."[49]

DOD and the Navy conducted studies on undersea warfare requirements in 2003-2004. One of the Navy studies—an internal Navy study done in 2004—reportedly recommended reducing the attack submarine force level requirement to as few as 37 boats. The study reportedly recommended homeporting a total of nine attack submarines at Guam and using satellites and unmanned underwater vehicles (UUVs) to perform ISR missions now performed by attack submarines.[50]

In March 2005, the Navy submitted to Congress a report projecting Navy force levels out to FY2035. The report presented two alternatives for FY2035—a 260-ship fleet including 37 SSNs and 4 SSGNs, and a 325-ship fleet including 41 SSNs and 4 SSGNs.[51]

In May 2005, it was reported that a newly completed DOD study on attack submarine requirements called for maintaining a force of 45 to 50 boats.[52]

In February 2006, the Navy proposed to maintain in coming years a fleet of 313 ships, including 48 SSNs. Some of the Navy's ship force-level goals have changed since 2006, and the goals now add up to a desired fleet of 328 ships. The figure of 48 SSNs, however, remains unchanged from 2006.

---

[48] Department of Navy point paper dated February 7, 2000. Reprinted in *Inside the Navy*, February 14, 2000, p. 5.

[49] U.S. Department of Defense, *Quadrennial Defense Review*, September 2001, p. 23.

[50] Bryan Bender, "Navy Eyes Cutting Submarine Force," *Boston Globe*, May 12, 2004, p. 1; Lolita C. Baldor, "Study Recommends Cutting Submarine Fleet," *NavyTimes.com*, May 13, 2004.

[51] U.S. Department of the Navy, *An Interim Report to Congress on Annual Long-Range Plan for the Construction of Naval Vessels for FY 2006*. The report was delivered to the House and Senate Armed Services and Appropriations Committees on March 23, 2005.

[52] Robert A. Hamilton, "Delegation Calls Report on Sub Needs Encouraging," *The Day (New London, CT)*, May 27, 2005; Jesse Hamilton, "Delegation to Get Details on Sub Report," *Hartford (CT) Courant*, May 26, 2005.

Appendix B. Options for Funding SSNs

This appendix presents information on some alternatives for funding SSNs that was originally incorporated into this report during discussions in earlier years on potential options for Virginia-class procurement.

Alternative Funding Methods

Alternative methods of funding the procurement of SSNs include but are not necessarily limited to the following:

- **two years of advance procurement funding followed by full funding**—the traditional approach, under which there are two years of advance procurement funding for the SSN's long-leadtime components, followed by the remainder of the boat's procurement funding in the year of procurement;

- **one year of advance procurement funding followed by full funding**—one year of advance procurement funding for the SSN's long-leadtime components, followed by the remainder of the boat's procurement funding in the year of procurement;

- **full funding with no advance procurement funding (single-year full funding)**—full funding of the SSN in the year of procurement, with no advance procurement funding in prior years;

- **incremental funding**—partial funding of the SSN in the year of procurement, followed by one or more years of additional funding increments needed to complete the procurement cost of the ship; and

- **advance appropriations**—a form of full funding that can be viewed as a legislatively locked in form of incremental funding.[53]

Navy testimony to Congress in early 2007, when Congress was considering the FY2008 budget, suggested that two years of advance procurement funding are required to fund the procurement of an SSN, and consequently that additional SSNs could not be procured until FY2010 at the earliest.[54] This testimony understated Congress's options regarding the procurement of additional SSNs in the near term. Although SSNs are normally procured with two years of advance procurement funding (which is used primarily for financing long-leadtime nuclear propulsion components), Congress can procure an SSN without prior-year advance procurement funding, or

---

[53] For additional discussion of these funding approaches, see CRS Report RL32776, *Navy Ship Procurement: Alternative Funding Approaches—Background and Options for Congress*, by Ronald O'Rourke.

[54] For example, at a March 1, 2007, hearing before the House Armed Services Committee on the FY2008 Department of the Navy budget request, Representative Taylor asked which additional ships the Navy might want to procure in FY2008, should additional funding be made available for that purpose. In response, Secretary of the Navy Donald Winter stated in part: "The Virginia-class submarines require us to start with a two-year advanced procurement, to be able to provide for the nuclear power plant that supports them. So we would need to start two years in advance. What that says is, if we were able to start in '08 with advanced procurement, we could accelerate, potentially, the two a year to 2010." (Source: Transcript of hearing.) Navy officials made similar statements before the same subcommittee on March 8, 2007, and before the Senate Armed Services Committee on March 29, 2007.

---

with only one year of advance procurement funding. Consequently, Congress at that time had option of procuring an additional SSN in FY2009 and/or FY2010.

Single-year full funding has been used in the past by Congress to procure nuclear-powered ships for which no prior-year advance procurement funding had been provided. Specifically, Congress used single-year full funding in FY1980 to procure the nuclear-powered aircraft carrier CVN-71, and again in FY1988 to procure the CVNs 74 and 75. In the case of the FY1988 procurement, under the Administration's proposed FY1988 budget, CVNs 74 and 75 were to be procured in FY1990 and FY1993, respectively, and the FY1988 budget was to make the initial advance procurement payment for CVN-74. Congress, in acting on the FY1988 budget, decided to accelerate the procurement of both ships to FY1988, and fully funded the two ships that year at a combined cost of $6.325 billion. The ships entered service in 1995 and 1998, respectively.[55]

The existence in both FY1980 and FY1988 of a spare set of Nimitz-class reactor components was not what made it possible for Congress to fund CVNs 71, 74, and 75 with single-year full funding; it simply permitted the ships to be built more quickly. What made it possible for Congress to fund the carriers with single-year full funding was Congress's constitutional authority to appropriate funding for that purpose.

Procuring an SSN with one year of advance procurement funding or no advance procurement funding would not materially change the way the SSN would be built—the process would still encompass about two years of advance work on long-leadtime components, and an additional six years or so of construction work on the ship itself. The outlay rate for the SSN could be slower, as outlays for construction of the ship itself would begin one or two years later than normal.

Congress in the past has procured certain ships in the knowledge that those ships would not begin construction for some time and consequently would take longer to enter service than a ship of that kind would normally require. When Congress procured two nuclear-powered aircraft carriers (CVNs 72 and 73) in FY1983, and another two (CVNs 74 and 75) in FY1988, it did so in both cases in the knowledge that the second ship in each case would not begin construction until some time after the first.

Procuring SSNs in a 2-1-2 Pattern

Some potential approaches for procuring additional boats in FY2009-FY2011 that were discussed in earlier years could have resulted in a pattern of procuring two boats in a given year, followed by one boat the following year, and two boats the year after that—a 2-1-2 pattern. Navy testimony to Congress in early 2007 and early 2008 suggested that if the procurement rate were increased in a given year to two boats, it would not be best, from an industrial-base point of view, to decrease the rate to a single boat the following year, and then increase it again to two boats the next year, because of the workforce fluctuations such a profile would produce.[56]

---

[55] In both FY1988 and FY1980, the Navy had a spare set of Nimitz (CVN-68) class nuclear propulsion components in inventory. The existence of a spare set of components permitted the carriers to be built more quickly than would have otherwise been the case, but it is not what made the single-year full funding of these carriers possible. What made it possible was Congress's authority to appropriate funds for the purpose.

[56] See, for example, the spoken remarks of Secretary of the Navy Donald Winter at hearings before the House Armed Services Committee on March 1, 2007, and March 6, 2008, and spoken remarks by other Navy officials at a March 29, 2007, hearing before the Senate Armed Services Committee and at a March 14, 2008, hearing before the Seapower and (continued...)

This statement may overstate the production-efficiency disadvantages of a 2-1-2 pattern. If two boats were procured in a given year, followed by one boat the next year—a total of three boats in 24 months—the schedule for producing the three boats could be phased so that, for a given stage in the production process, the production rate would be one boat every eight months. A production rate of one boat every 8 months might actually help the industrial base make the transition from the current schedule of one boat every 12 months (one boat per year) to one boat every 6 months (two boats per year). Viewed this way, a 2-1-2 pattern might actually lead to some benefits in production efficiency on the way to a steady rate of two boats per year. The Navy's own FY2009 30-year (FY2009-FY2038) SSN procurement plan called for procuring SSNs in a 1-2-1-2 pattern in FY2029-FY2038.

Author Contact Information

Ronald O'Rourke
Specialist in Naval Affairs
rorourke@crs.loc.gov, 7-7610

(...continued)
Expeditionary Forces subcommittee of the House Armed Services Committee.
